HARRIET TUBMAN

BOOK FOR CURIOUS KIDS

Exploring the Inspiring Life of a
Courageous Freedom Fighter for
the Liberty of Others

TIMOTHY STARLYN

TABLE OF CONTENTS

INTRODUCTION

Have you ever wondered what it would be like to escape from a life of slavery? To journey through darkness, guided by the light of hope and courage? Harriet Tubman knew this journey all too well.

Imagine growing up in a world where your future is not your own. Where families are torn apart, and freedom seems like a distant dream. Harriet Tubman's life story is one of resilience, bravery, and unwavering determination—a story that has inspired generations.

In this book, we'll delve into the remarkable life of Harriet Tubman, a woman who defied all odds to lead enslaved people to freedom. From her early years filled with struggle and hardship to her courageous exploits on the Underground Railroad, Harriet's journey is nothing short of extraordinary.

Each chapter in this book unveils a different aspect of Harriet Tubman's life and legacy. We'll explore her childhood experiences, her visions of hope, and the challenges she faced as she fought for freedom. We'll witness her unwavering commitment to family and the risks she took to guide others to safety.

Join us as we discover the seeds of courage that grew within Harriet Tubman, shaping her into one of history's most revered heroes.

Through the lens of her extraordinary life, we'll uncover valuable lessons that can inspire us all—lessons of courage, perseverance, and the relentless pursuit of freedom. Harriet Tubman's legacy continues to echo through time, reminding us of the strength that resides within each of us.

Get ready to embark on a captivating journey through history—a journey that celebrates Harriet Tubman's indomitable spirit and enduring quest for equality and liberation. Let her story ignite your imagination and inspire you to stand strong in the face of adversity.

Are you ready to discover the remarkable life of Harriet Tubman? Let's begin this extraordinary adventure together.

Seeds of Courage

Once upon a time, in the quiet shadows of a sprawling plantation near the Blackwater River in Maryland, a remarkable girl named Minty lived with her family. Minty's full name was Araminta "Minty" Ross, but everyone called her Minty for short. She was born into slavery, a life where freedom was a dream whispered under the cover of night.

Minty's parents, Rit and Ben Ross were enslaved by different families on the same plantation. Rit worked as a cook for the Brodess family, while Ben was a skilled woodsman managing timber work for another owner named Anthony Thompson. Minty was the fifth of nine children born to Rit and

Ben, but their lives were not their own. The Brodess family, especially Edward Brodess, who owned Minty's mother, made their lives full of hardship and uncertainty.

The exact date of Minty's birth is a mystery. Some say it was in 1822, while others believe it might have been earlier. It was a time when enslaved families like Minty's were kept apart, sold off, and subjected to cruel treatment. Rit, Minty's mother, fought desperately to protect her children. When traders came looking to sell Minty's younger brother, Moses, Rit hid him for a whole month, sheltered by others who despised the injustice of slavery.

Rit's fierce determination to keep her family together left a deep mark on Minty's heart. She witnessed her mother's bravery when Rit boldly confronted Edward Brodess. Startled by Rit's defiance, Brodess backed down, and the sale of Minty's brother Moses was ultimately abandoned.

These stories of resistance and resilience stayed with Minty as she grew. She saw the strength in her mother's eyes and learned the power of standing up against injustice. As Minty grew older, she began to dream of a world where her people could be free.

Minty's family history was a blend of courage and struggle. Her grandmother, Modesty, had been brought to America on a ship from Africa, a distant memory buried in the shadows of history. Minty was told she possessed the spirit of an Ashanti person, a reminder of her unknown heritage.

Despite the darkness of slavery, Minty's spirit remained unbroken. She inherited her father's woodsmanship and her mother's determination. Little did she know that one day, she would escape the plantation and embark on a journey that would transform her into a legendary figure of freedom.

As the days passed on the plantation, Minty dreamed of a life beyond the cotton fields and the watchful eyes of her oppressors. She believed in a future where families like hers could live in freedom, where no child would be torn from their mother's arms.

Growing Up Strong

Minty, whose real name was Araminta, but everyone called her Minty for short, had a tough start in life. Her mother, Rit, was often busy working in "the big house," leaving Minty to care for her younger siblings on the plantation. This was common for many children in large enslaved families like hers.

When Minty was just five or six years old, Edward Brodess, the man who owned her and her family, hired her out to work as a nursemaid for a woman named Miss Susan. Minty's job was to take care of Miss Susan's baby, rocking the cradle until it fell asleep. But if the baby woke up and cried, Minty would be punished with a whipping. Minty endured this cruelty day after day, sometimes receiving five lashes before breakfast. The scars from these beatings would stay with her for the rest of her life.

Despite the pain, Minty found ways to resist. Once, she ran away for five days, seeking a brief escape from the harsh reality of her life. She also learned to protect herself by wearing extra layers of clothing to lessen the impact of the beatings, and she even fought back against those who tried to hurt her.

As Minty grew older, her life did not get easier. She was sent to work for another planter named James Cook, who made her check muskrat traps in the nearby marshes. Even when Minty contracted measles and became seriously ill, Cook still forced her to work. It was only when Minty's condition worsened that Cook sent her back to Brodess, where her mother, Rit, nursed her back to health.

Throughout her challenging childhood, Minty felt a deep sense of homesickness and longing for freedom. She often compared herself to a character in a song called "Old Folks at Home," feeling isolated and far from where she truly belonged.

As Minty grew stronger, her tasks on the plantation became harder. She was assigned to tough jobs like working in the fields, driving oxen, plowing the land, and hauling heavy logs. Despite the backbreaking labor and constant hardships, Minty's spirit remained unbroken. She dreamed of a day when she could be free and live a life of her own choosing.

TIMOTHY STARLYN

Visions of Hope

In her adolescent years, young Minty faced a tragic accident that changed her life forever. One day, as she worked in the fields, an overseer hurled a heavy metal weight—intended for another fleeing enslaved person—at Minty. The weight struck her head with such force that it "broke my skull," as she later recalled. Bleeding and unconscious, Minty was carried back to her owner's house and left on the seat of a loom without any medical care for two agonizing days.

After this terrible incident, Minty suffered from excruciating headaches and began to have seizures that caused her to seemingly lose consciousness. Despite this, Minty remained aware of her surroundings even when she appeared to be asleep. Historians have speculated about the cause of these seizures, suggesting they might have been related to a type of epilepsy or another neurological condition triggered by her head injury.

However, it was during this time of suffering that Minty began to experience something extraordinary—visions and vivid dreams that she believed were messages from God. These spiritual encounters profoundly impacted Minty's character and strengthened her faith. Although she couldn't read or write, Minty learned Bible stories from her mother and attended a Methodist church with her family. The tales of deliverance and resistance in the Old Testament resonated deeply with Minty, shaping her beliefs and guiding her actions.

Minty rejected the teachings of white preachers who preached passivity and obedience to enslaved people. Instead, she found inspiration in the stories of Moses leading the Israelites out of slavery and other biblical figures who defied tyranny. Minty believed that God was calling her to a greater purpose—a purpose that would lead her to fight for freedom and justice.

Despite her struggles and the limitations imposed by her condition, Minty's unwavering faith sustained her. She drew strength from her spiritual experiences and believed that God had chosen her for a special mission.

As Minty grew into a young woman, her resolve to defy oppression and lead others to freedom would only strengthen. Her faith in God's guidance would become the cornerstone of her extraordinary journey—

a journey that would eventually see her transform from Minty, the girl with a broken skull, into Harriet Tubman, the courageous conductor of the Underground Railroad.

And so, dear readers, remember the strength and conviction that Minty drew from her faith. Even in the darkest of times, she never lost sight of her calling—to lead her people out of bondage and into the light of freedom.

Hope, Marriage, and Courage

In the 1840s, on the Eastern Shore of Maryland, Harriet Tubman's life took a new turn. After years of hardship and suffering, a glimmer of hope emerged when her father, Ben Ross, was promised freedom at the age of 45 by his owner, Anthony Thompson. When Thompson passed away, his son honored this promise in 1840, granting Ben his long-awaited freedom. Despite gaining his freedom, Ben chose to continue working as a timber estimator and foreman for the Thompson family, demonstrating resilience and determination.

Meanwhile, Harriet faced her own struggles. Determined to uncover the truth about her mother, Rit's, legal status, Harriet scraped together five dollars—an impressive sum at the time—to hire a white attorney. Through this investigation, Harriet discovered that according to a will left by Atthow Pattison, the grandfather of Mary Brodess (the woman who owned Harriet and her family), Rit and her children were supposed to be set free at age 45. However, the Pattison and Brodess families had ignored this promise, and challenging their power was a daunting task for Harriet.

Around 1844, Harriet married John Tubman, a free black man. This marriage was complicated by Harriet's enslaved status because, according to the law at the time, the status of children followed that of their mother—meaning any children born to Harriet and John would be born into slavery. Despite these challenges, such unions between free people of color and enslaved individuals were not uncommon on the Eastern Shore of Maryland, where families often included both free and enslaved members.

After her marriage, Harriet decided to change her name from Araminta to Harriet, adopting her mother's name as a way to honor her family and possibly as part of a newfound religious conviction. Some historians believe this name change was connected to Harriet's plans to escape from slavery, signifying a symbolic rebirth and a break from her past.

Harriet Tubman's marriage and name change marked a significant chapter in her life. Despite the obstacles she faced as an enslaved woman, Harriet remained determined to seek freedom not only for herself but also for her loved ones. Her resilience and courage would soon lead her down a path that would change the course of history.

As Harriet's story unfolds, dear readers, remember her unwavering spirit and her relentless pursuit of freedom. Each step she took, and each decision she made was a testament to her strength and her unwavering belief in a better future.

Prayers for Freedom

In the year 1849, Harriet Tubman faced yet another trial in her life. Falling ill once more, Harriet's value to slave traders decreased, and Edward Brodess, her owner, attempted to sell her. However, to his frustration, he couldn't find a buyer. Angry and determined to change her situation, Harriet turned to prayer, seeking guidance and strength from God.

Night after night, Harriet prayed fervently, pleading for a change in Edward Brodess's heart. Her prayers intensified as Brodess continued to bring people to look at her and attempt to sell her like property.

Remarkably, just a week after Harriet's impassioned prayers, Edward Brodess passed away. Harriet, who had wished for change but not this kind of change, expressed regret for her earlier sentiments. However, with Brodess's death, the future became even more uncertain for Harriet and her family.

Following Edward Brodess's demise, his widow, Eliza, set out to sell the enslaved individuals who had been part of the estate settlement. Seeing her family on the brink of being torn apart once again, Harriet refused to wait for someone else to decide her fate. Despite her husband's efforts to dissuade her, Harriet knew she had to take action.

With unwavering resolve, Harriet declared, "There was one of two things I had a right to, liberty or death; if I could not have one,

I would have the other." Alongside her brothers, Ben and Henry, Harriet made the daring decision to escape from slavery on September 17, 1849.

At that time, Harriet had been hired out by Anthony Thompson, who owned a large plantation in Poplar Neck, Caroline County. It is likely that her brothers also labored for Thompson. Because they were hired out, Eliza Brodess did not immediately recognize their absence as an escape attempt.

Two weeks passed before Eliza Brodess posted a runaway notice in the local newspaper, offering a substantial reward for the capture and return of each escapee. Despite the risk and the mounting pressure, Harriet's brothers began to have second thoughts. Ben, perhaps troubled by leaving behind his wife and children, convinced both Harriet and Henry to return with him.

The return was not what Harriet had hoped for. She knew deep down that the longing for freedom burned brighter than ever in her heart. Harriet Tubman's story was far from over. Her journey toward liberty would continue, fueled by her unyielding spirit and unwavering determination to secure freedom for herself and those she loved.

As we reflect on Harriet's courageous decision to escape, let us remember the strength of her convictions and the sacrifices she made in pursuit of a life of liberty. Harriet Tubman's legacy teaches us that even in the face of overwhelming adversity, the human spirit can triumph with courage and resilience.

Escaping to the Promised Land

In the chilly months of October or November, Harriet Tubman made a daring escape from slavery once again, this time without her brothers by her side. Before leaving, she cleverly hinted at her plans by singing a farewell song to Mary, a trusted friend: "I'll meet you in the morning. I'm bound for the promised land." These words were not just a song but a coded message expressing Harriet's determination to reach freedom.

Harriet's exact path to freedom remains a mystery. Still, she relied on the Underground Railroad—a secret network of courageous individuals composed of free and enslaved black people, white abolitionists, and activists dedicated to helping enslaved people escape to freedom. Quakers played a significant role in this network in Maryland. Harriet likely sought refuge first in the Preston area near Poplar Neck, where a substantial Quaker community provided support and shelter.

From there, Harriet embarked on a perilous journey northeast along the Choptank River, through Delaware, and eventually into Pennsylvania—a journey of nearly 90 miles on foot that could take anywhere from five days to three weeks. Traveling only by night and guided by the North Star, Harriet had to evade slave catchers eager to capture and return fugitive slaves for rewards.

The Underground Railroad conductors used clever tactics to protect Harriet and others escaping slavery. At one stop, the lady of the house instructed Harriet to sweep the yard during the day, creating the appearance that she was a hired worker. When night fell, the family concealed Harriet in a cart and safely transported her to the next friendly household along the route. During the day, Harriet likely sought refuge in the familiar woods and marshes of the region, hiding from those who would send her back into bondage.

The specifics of Harriet's first journey to freedom are shrouded in secrecy, as she knew the importance of keeping these routes hidden to protect future escapees. Nevertheless, Harriet's determination and resourcefulness guided her across the border into Pennsylvania.

Upon realizing she had crossed into free territory, Harriet felt an overwhelming sense of relief and wonder. She described the moment years later, saying, "When I found I had crossed that line, I looked at my hands to see if I was the same person. There was such a glory over everything; the sun came like gold through the trees and over the fields, and I felt like I was in Heaven."

Harriet Tubman's escape marked a pivotal moment in her life—a moment of liberation and profound joy. Her journey to freedom was just beginning, but with each step, she drew closer to a new life filled with hope and possibility. Harriet's courage and determination continue to inspire us today, reminding us of the power of resilience in the face of adversity.

Fighting for Family Freedom

After Harriet Tubman reached Philadelphia, a new chapter of her incredible journey began. Despite the freedom she now enjoyed, Harriet felt a deep longing for her family back in Maryland. "I was a stranger in a strange land," she later recalled. "My father, my mother, my brothers, and sisters, and friends were [in Maryland]. But I was free, and they should be free too."

Determined to reunite her family and help them find the same freedom she had discovered, Harriet worked tirelessly at odd jobs in Philadelphia and Cape May, New Jersey, saving every penny she could. But during this time, a new threat emerged—the

U.S. Congress passed the Fugitive Slave Act of 1850. This law required law enforcement officials, even in states where slavery was outlawed, to assist in capturing escaped slaves and imposed severe punishments for anyone caught aiding their escape. This made life even more dangerous for those who had fled slavery.

Racial tensions were also rising in Philadelphia as poor Irish immigrants competed with free blacks for jobs, adding to the challenges faced by Harriet and others seeking a new life.

In December 1850, Harriet received a distressing message that her niece Kessiah and Kessiah's children were about to be sold into slavery in Cambridge, Maryland. Without hesitation, Harriet traveled to Baltimore, where her brother-in-law, Tom Tubman, hid her until the day of the sale.

Kessiah's husband, John Bowley, a free black man, devised a daring plan—he made the winning bid for his wife at the auction. While the auctioneer took a break for lunch, John, Kessiah, and their children escaped to a nearby safe house. When night fell, John skillfully sailed his family 60 miles on a log canoe to Baltimore, where Harriet awaited them. Together, they journeyed to Philadelphia, where Kessiah and her children were finally safe and free.

In the early months of the following year, Harriet returned to Maryland on a mission to rescue more family members. During this second trip, she successfully guided her youngest brother, Moses, and two other men to freedom. News of Harriet's courageous exploits spread, inspiring her family and strengthening her resolve with each perilous journey back into Maryland.

Harriet Tubman's unwavering determination and bravery knew no bounds. Despite the risks and challenges she faced, she never wavered in her quest to reunite her family and liberate those still bound by the chains of slavery. Harriet's story is a testament to the power of hope, courage, and the enduring love of family. As she continued her heroic efforts, Harriet would leave an indelible mark on history, forever changing the lives of those she rescued and inspiring generations to come.

Guiding Others to Freedom Amid Personal Challenges

In late 1851, Harriet Tubman returned to Dorchester County, Maryland, for the first time since her daring escape. This time, her mission was to find her husband, John. However, upon her arrival, Harriet discovered that John had married another woman named Caroline. Despite her disappointment and hurt, Harriet reached out to John, urging him to join her in freedom. But John insisted that he was content where he was, choosing to remain with Caroline.

Suppressing her anger and sadness, Harriet focused on helping others who shared her desire for freedom. She connected with enslaved individuals who also longed to escape the bonds of slavery and led them on a dangerous journey to Philadelphia—a city where they could find safety and freedom.

During this time, the Fugitive Slave Law had made the northern United States increasingly perilous for those seeking freedom. Harriet realized that many escapees, including those she had helped rescue, were migrating northward to Southern Ontario, Canada, where slavery had been abolished.

In December 1851, Harriet courageously guided a group of 11 escapees, possibly including the Bowleys and others she had previously rescued, on a northward journey. Evidence suggests that Harriet and her group sought refuge at the home of the renowned abolitionist Frederick Douglass, who was himself a former enslaved person.

Frederick Douglass and Harriet Tubman shared a deep admiration for each other's tireless efforts in the fight against slavery. In a letter to Harriet, Douglass expressed his profound respect, contrasting their approaches to activism. He acknowledged that while he had worked publicly and received encouragement, Harriet had labored tirelessly in the shadows of night, facing countless dangers and hardships.

Douglass praised Harriet's unwavering dedication and heroism, comparing her commitment to freedom to that of John Brown, a revered abolitionist. He recognized Harriet's sacrifices, highlighting her bravery in the face of adversity.

TIMOTHY STARLYN

Guiding Parents to Freedom

During the years from 1851 to 1862, Harriet Tubman embarked on numerous daring expeditions back to the Eastern Shore of Maryland. Her goal? To rescue enslaved individuals seeking freedom—over 70 in about 13 remarkable missions.

Among those Harriet rescued were her own brothers—Henry, Ben, and Robert—along with their wives and some of their children. Harriet didn't just lead people to freedom; she also provided detailed instructions to another 50 to 60 enslaved individuals who managed to escape on their own, thanks to her guidance.

Harriet's courageous actions earned her a powerful nickname: "Moses," a reference to the biblical leader who guided the Hebrews to freedom from Egypt. Like Moses, Harriet fearlessly led her people to a promised land of liberty.

One of Harriet's most poignant missions was to rescue her aging parents, who were still living in a hostile and dangerous environment even after gaining their freedom. In 1855, Harriet's father, Ben Ross, purchased her mother, Rit, from Eliza Brodess. Despite this, the area remained unsafe for free Black individuals.

In 1857, Harriet received alarming news— her father was in danger of arrest for sheltering a group of eight people escaping from slavery. Without hesitation, Harriet made plans to bring her parents to Canada safely.

With bravery and determination, Harriet guided her parents north to St. Catharines, Canada, where a supportive community of formerly enslaved individuals had gathered. Here, Harriet's parents could finally find peace and security, surrounded by friends and relatives who had also escaped the horrors of slavery.

Harriet Tubman's extraordinary efforts and unwavering commitment to freedom changed countless lives. Her selfless acts of courage and compassion paved the way for so many to experience the joys of liberty.

TIMOTHY STARLYN

Master of Escape

Harriet Tubman was a woman of extraordinary courage and resourcefulness. Her dangerous work rescuing enslaved people required not only bravery but also clever tactics and unwavering faith.

She carefully planned her missions during winter, when long nights and cold weather helped conceal her movements. Harriet would start her escapes on Saturday evenings, knowing that runaway notices wouldn't appear in newspapers until Monday morning, giving her a crucial head start.

To avoid detection, Harriet used clever disguises and quick thinking. Once, while disguised with a bonnet and carrying live chickens, she unexpectedly encountered a former enslaver. Thinking fast, Harriet agitated the chickens, diverting attention and allowing her to pass without raising suspicion.

On another occasion, when she recognized a former enslaver on a train, Harriet grabbed a nearby newspaper and pretended to read despite being illiterate. Her quick actions helped her avoid unwanted attention.

During an interview in 1897, Harriet shared details of her daring journeys along the Underground Railroad. She sought refuge with kind individuals like Sam Green, a free black minister, and hid near her parents' home at Poplar Neck in Maryland.

Her journey continued northeast through Delaware, guided by trusted allies like William and Nat Brinkley and Abraham Gibbs. Harriet traveled across challenging terrain, relying on safe houses and networks of abolitionists to reach freedom.

Harriet's deep faith sustained her during these dangerous missions. She believed her childhood visions were divine messages guiding her path. Harriet often prayed and trusted that God would protect her.

Thomas Garrett, a Quaker abolitionist, provided critical support in Wilmington, securing transportation to safety in Philadelphia. Harriet's reliance on God and spirituals, like "Go Down Moses," served as coded messages to fellow travelers, signaling danger or safety.

Armed with a revolver for protection against slave catchers, Harriet was determined to keep her passengers safe. She once confronted a man who wanted to turn back, pointing her gun and urging him to continue. Her resolute actions ensured everyone reached their destination.

By the late 1850s, slaveholders held public meetings to address the growing number of escapes. Little did they know that the petite woman known as "Minty" was behind so many successful rescues.

Despite rumors of hefty rewards for her capture, Harriet and her passengers evaded capture. She proudly declared, "I never ran my train off the track, and I never lost a passenger."

Fighting for Freedom

In April 1858, Harriet Tubman crossed paths with a passionate abolitionist named John Brown. Unlike others who advocated peaceful methods, Brown believed in using force to end slavery. Harriet admired Brown's direct approach and shared his belief that God called them to fight against slavery.

When Brown started recruiting supporters for an attack on slaveholders, he welcomed Harriet into his fold, calling her "General Tubman." Harriet's knowledge of the support networks in Pennsylvania, Maryland,

and Delaware proved invaluable to Brown's plans.

John Brown dreamed of sparking a rebellion that would lead to a new state for freed slaves. He envisioned starting a battle that would inspire enslaved people across the South to rise against their oppressors. He asked Harriet to gather former slaves from Southern Ontario who might join his cause.

On May 8, 1858, Brown unveiled his plan for a raid on Harpers Ferry, Virginia, at a meeting in Chatham, Canada. However, when news of the plan leaked, Brown postponed the raid to raise more funds and refine his strategy. Harriet assisted him during this critical time.

While Brown prepared for the attack in October 1859, Harriet fell ill in New

Bedford, Massachusetts. Although it's unclear if she still intended to join Brown's raid, by the time of the Harpers Ferry raid on October 16, Harriet had recovered in New York City.

Unfortunately, the raid did not succeed. John Brown was arrested, tried for treason and murder, and eventually executed on December 2. Despite the failed mission, Brown's actions inspired many abolitionists who saw him as a hero willing to sacrifice everything for freedom.

Harriet Tubman admired Brown's courage and commitment, believing that his sacrifice had a profound impact on the fight against slavery. She praised his bravery, saying he had accomplished more in his death than most could in a lifetime.

Harriet Tubman's involvement with John Brown highlighted her dedication to the cause of freedom. Though their plan did not succeed, their shared vision and unwavering resolve left a lasting legacy in the fight against slavery.

A Safe Haven and Last Rescue

In early 1859, Harriet Tubman bought a seven-acre farm in Fleming, New York, near the bustling city of Auburn. The area was filled with people who opposed slavery, making it a perfect place for Harriet to live and continue her work.

Tubman's farm became a sanctuary for her family and friends. She often took in relatives and others seeking freedom in the North, providing them with a safe place to stay. Harriet's determination to help others never wavered.

Not long after settling into her new home, Tubman returned to Maryland to bring back a young girl named Margaret. Harriet claimed Margaret was her niece and that her parents were free. Margaret later described her childhood home as prosperous, but her sudden move raised questions among historians about Harriet's true intentions.

In November 1860, Harriet embarked on her final rescue mission. For years, she had tried to free her sister Rachel and her children, Ben and Angerine, from slavery. Sadly, Rachel had passed away by the time Harriet returned. To rescue her niece and nephew, Harriet needed $30, but she didn't have the money. Heartbroken, she couldn't save them, and their fate remains unknown.

Despite this setback, Harriet never gave up. During her journey back to New York, she led another group of escapees, including the Ennalls family, to safety. They faced harsh weather and hunger, but Harriet's bravery and quick thinking ensured they reached their destination.

On December 28, 1860, Harriet and her group arrived at the home of David and Martha Wright in Auburn. The journey had been difficult, but Harriet was relieved that everyone was safe.

Harriet Tubman's new farm in New York became a beacon of hope for those seeking freedom. Her unwavering courage and determination inspired countless others to fight against slavery and injustice. Despite the challenges she faced, Harriet's legacy of compassion and bravery continues to inspire people around the world.

TIMOTHY STARLYN

Finding Freedom in War

When the Civil War broke out in 1861, Harriet had a vision that the war would soon lead to the abolition of slavery. More immediately, enslaved people near Union positions began escaping in large numbers.

General Benjamin Butler declared these escapees to be "contraband" – property seized by northern forces – and put them to work, initially without pay, at Fort Monroe in Virginia. The number of "contrabands" encamped at Fort Monroe and other Union positions rapidly increased.

In January 1862, Harriet volunteered to support the Union cause and began helping refugees in the camps, particularly in Port Royal, South Carolina.

In South Carolina, Harriet met General David Hunter, a strong supporter of abolition. He declared all of the "contrabands" in the Port Royal district free and began gathering formerly enslaved people for a regiment of black soldiers. U.S. President Abraham Lincoln was not yet prepared to enforce emancipation in the southern states, so he reprimanded Hunter for his actions.

Harriet condemned Lincoln's response and his general unwillingness to consider ending slavery in the U.S. for both moral and practical reasons:

Harriet served as a nurse in Port Royal, preparing remedies from local plants and aiding soldiers suffering from dysentery and infectious diseases. At first, she received government rations for her work, but to dispel a perception that she was getting special treatment, she gave up her right to these supplies and made money selling pies and root beer, which she made in the evenings.

Leading the Way to Freedom

When President Lincoln issued the Emancipation Proclamation, Harriet saw it as a step forward but believed there was more to be done to free all black people from slavery. She dedicated herself to direct actions against the Confederacy.

In early 1863, Harriet used her skills in covert travel and reconnaissance to lead a group of scouts around Port Royal. Under the orders of Secretary of War Edwin Stanton, her team mapped the unfamiliar terrain and gathered intelligence about the area's inhabitants. Harriet later worked alongside Colonel James Montgomery, providing crucial information that helped capture Jacksonville, Florida.

Later that year, Harriet played a pivotal role in the daring raid at Combahee Ferry. She guided three steamboats filled with black soldiers commanded by Colonel Montgomery up the Combahee River, past dangerous mines, to assault several plantations. Once ashore, Union troops set fire to the plantations, destroying infrastructure and seizing valuable supplies. Harriet's spy network had warned enslaved people in the area about the raid, and they heard the steamboats' whistles signaling their liberation.

Harriet witnessed a chaotic scene as men, women, and children stampeded toward the boats, carrying whatever they could, from pots of rice to squealing pigs. Despite armed overseers trying to stop them, the mass escape was unstoppable. Over 750 formerly enslaved people made it onto the steamboats, heading toward freedom in Beaufort.

Newspapers praised Harriet's bravery and intelligence in the raid, calling her a patriot with remarkable abilities. They also praised her recruiting efforts, as over 100 of the newly liberated men joined the Union army. Harriet's involvement in the raid revived her nickname, "General Tubman," given to her by John Brown years earlier.

Reports credited Harriet as the first woman to lead U.S. troops in an armed assault, though her exact contributions have sometimes been exaggerated.

In July 1863, Harriet assisted Colonel Robert Gould Shaw during the assault on

Fort Wagner. She reportedly served him his last meal before the battle. Harriet vividly described the intensity of the battle to historian Albert Bushnell Hart, comparing the gunfire to lightning and the falling rain to the drops of blood shed in battle.

For two more years, Harriet continued her important work for the Union forces, caring for newly liberated people, scouting Confederate territory, and nursing wounded soldiers in Virginia even after the Confederacy surrendered in April 1865. Her courage and dedication left a lasting impact on the fight for freedom during the Civil War.

Standing Strong Through Hardship

After years of brave service to the Union during the Civil War, Harriet Tubman received very little pay for her efforts. She wasn't officially recognized as a soldier and was only occasionally compensated for her work as a spy and scout. Her nursing work was entirely unpaid. Despite over three years of service, she received only a total of $200, which was not enough for all she had done.

Because she wasn't officially recognized, documenting her service was difficult. The U.S. government was slow to acknowledge her contributions or pay her what she deserved. Meanwhile, Harriet's focus remained on helping her family and those who were formerly enslaved, which kept her in a state of constant poverty.

In July 1865, a promised position as a military nurse fell through. Disheartened, Harriet decided to return to her home in New York. During her train ride in October 1865, she faced discrimination and mistreatment. Despite being entitled to a half-fare ticket due to her service, a conductor demanded she move to the less desirable smoking car. When she refused, he cursed at her and forcibly moved her, injuring her in the process. White passengers joined in, cursing at her and demanding she be kicked off the train.

Back in Auburn, New York, Harriet spent her remaining years caring for her family and others in need. Alongside managing her farm, she took in boarders and worked various jobs to make ends meet and support her elderly parents.

One of the boarders Harriet took in was Nelson Davis, a farmer and former soldier who had served in the United States Colored Infantry Regiment. Despite their 22-year age difference, Harriet and Nelson fell in love. They were married on March 18, 1869, at the Central Presbyterian Church in Auburn. The couple later adopted a baby girl named Gertie in 1874, filling their home with love and joy.

Throughout her life, Harriet Tubman faced immense challenges but always stood strong. Her courage, compassion, and determination continue to inspire people to this day.

A Story of Family, Farming, and Legacy

In 1859, Harriet Tubman settled into a new life in Auburn, New York, on land that she had purchased from William H. Seward. This place would become more than just a home—it would be a sanctuary for her family and friends.

One day in 1866, a man named Nelson Davis arrived in Auburn and became a boarder in Harriet's house. Nelson had a remarkable story of his own. He was originally known as Nelson Charles, having worked for a family named Charles. Nelson likely escaped slavery around 1861, possibly using the Underground

Railroad to navigate to freedom. After his escape, he changed his last name to Davis, adopting his father's surname, Milford Davis. By 1861, Nelson had made his way to Oneida County, New York, where he lived.

During the Civil War, around 1863, Nelson enlisted in the Union Army and fought bravely for freedom. After the war ended, he was discharged in Texas, having served his country with honor.

In time, Nelson and Harriet's bond deepened, and they were married on March 18, 1869, at the Central Presbyterian Church. Despite their age difference—Nelson was more than twenty years younger than Harriet—their marriage was built on love and shared values.

Together, Harriet and Nelson operated a thriving farm and brick business on their 7-acre property in Auburn. They tended to chickens and pigs, grew potatoes, vegetables, and apples, and sold butter and eggs. Their home was also a place of refuge for others, with boarders and family members finding shelter and support under their roof.

In the early 1880s, tragedy struck when their wooden house was destroyed by fire. Undeterred, they rebuilt their home, this time using brick, which was more resilient to fire.

During this challenging time, Nelson fell seriously ill with tuberculosis. Harriet took on the role of caregiver, tending to her husband's needs and managing the farm and business single-handedly.

Sadly, Nelson Davis passed away in 1888 due to his illness. Harriet, now known as Harriet Tubman Davis, applied for pension benefits available to Civil War veterans' spouses.

Despite the hardships she faced, Harriet Tubman continued to embody resilience and determination. She endured loss and adversity with unwavering strength, carrying on the legacy of courage that defined her remarkable life.

Overcoming Challenges

Despite her heroic actions during the Civil War, Harriet Tubman faced financial struggles in her later years. Fortunately, her friends and supporters from her abolitionist days rallied to help her.

In October of that same year, Harriet fell victim to a cruel scam. Two men claimed to have access to a trunk of gold coins smuggled out of South Carolina by a former slave. They offered to sell the coins to Harriet for less than half of their value. Harriet, believing their story was true, borrowed money from a friend and arranged to meet the men late at night to receive the gold. However, when they met in the woods, the men knocked Harriet out with chloroform and stole her purse. To Harriet's dismay, the trunk they gave her was filled with rocks instead of gold coins. This incident highlighted Harriet's financial vulnerability and prompted local leaders to take notice of her precarious situation.

In 1874, two U.S. Representatives, Clinton D. MacDougall of New York and Gerry W. Hazelton of Wisconsin, proposed a bill to pay Harriet $2,000 for her services to the Union Army as a scout, nurse, and spy. Unfortunately, the bill was defeated in the Senate. Despite setbacks, Harriet's supporters remained dedicated to helping her. When her wooden house burned down in February 1880, they rallied together to build her a new brick home.

Tragedy struck again in 1888 when Harriet's beloved husband, Nelson Davis, passed away from tuberculosis. His death made Harriet eligible for a pension as his widow under the Dependent and Disability Pension Act of 1890. After providing documentation of her marriage and her husband's military service, Harriet was granted a widow's pension of $8 per month, along with a lump sum of $500 to cover the delayed approval.

In 1897, Congressman Sereno E. Payne introduced a bill to grant Harriet a soldier's monthly pension of $25, which reflected her service as a nurse and her contributions to the war effort. Despite objections from some members of Congress, Harriet eventually received a compromise amount of $20 per month. This pension recognized her dedication and sacrifices, although it did not fully acknowledge her role as a scout and spy.

Throughout her life, Harriet Tubman showed incredible strength and resilience in the face of adversity. Her story inspires us to persevere and stand up for what is right, no matter the challenges we may encounter.

Championing Women's Rights

As Harriet Tubman grew older, she continued her fight for equality by advocating for women's right to vote. When asked by a white woman whether women should have the right to vote, Harriet responded, "I suffered enough to believe it." This powerful statement reflected her belief that women, like men, deserved the right to participate in shaping their country's future.

Harriet began attending meetings of suffragist organizations and working alongside notable women such as Susan B. Anthony and Emily Howland. Together, they traveled to cities like New York, Boston, and Washington, D.C., where Harriet spoke passionately in support of women's voting rights. She shared stories of her experiences during and after the Civil War, emphasizing the important roles women played in shaping history.

In 1896, Harriet Tubman was the keynote speaker at the inaugural meeting of the National Federation of Afro-American Women. Her presence and powerful words inspired many to join the movement for women's suffrage.

Harriet's activism gained recognition in the press, with publications like The Woman's Era featuring her in a series of articles titled "Eminent Women." This spotlight helped elevate Harriet's profile and brought attention to her lifelong dedication to advancing the rights of others.

Despite her influential contributions, Harriet Tubman remained in poverty due to her selfless devotion to helping others. When invited to receptions and celebrations in her honor, Harriet had to sell a cow to afford a train ticket to attend these events. Her sacrifices and commitment to social change were a testament to her unwavering spirit and determination.

Harriet Tubman's efforts as a suffragist were rooted in her belief that every person, regardless of gender or background, deserved equal rights and opportunities. Her advocacy laid the groundwork for future generations of women to continue the fight for equality and justice.

The Last Chapter

In the 1870s, Harriet Tubman became an active member of the Thompson Memorial African Methodist Episcopal (AME) Zion Church in Auburn. She cared deeply about her community and, in 1895, began discussions to establish a home for elderly and needy African Americans. Despite her own financial struggles, Harriet bid at an auction and purchased a 25-acre farm adjacent to her own to serve as the site for this new facility.

To honor her friend and fellow abolitionist John Brown, Harriet named one of the buildings on the farm "John Brown Hall."

However, fundraising for the project proved challenging, and Harriet faced difficulties with mortgage loans. Eventually, the AME Zion Church took over the property in 1903, but the home did not open until five years later due to ongoing financial obstacles.

When the home finally opened in 1908, Harriet was frustrated by a new rule requiring residents to pay an entrance fee. She believed the home should welcome those with no money at all. Despite her concerns, she was a guest of honor at the opening celebration.

As Harriet grew older, she continued to suffer from the effects of a childhood head injury. In the late 1890s, she sought relief by undergoing a risky operation at a hospital in Boston. Without anesthesia, she endured the procedure, likening her experience to Civil War soldiers who endured amputations.

Despite the challenges, she found some comfort afterward.

By 1911, Harriet's health declined significantly, and she was admitted to the rest home named in her honor. Reports of her illness and financial struggles prompted an outpouring of support from her supporters. Surrounded by loved ones, Harriet Tubman passed away on March 10, 1913, from pneumonia.

Before her death, Harriet shared a poignant message from the Gospel of John with those by her side: "I go away to prepare a place for you." Her burial at Fort Hill Cemetery in Auburn was marked with semi-military honors, a fitting tribute to a woman whose bravery, compassion, and dedication left an indelible mark on American history.

Harriet Tubman's legacy lives on in the stories of her courage and determination, inspiring generations to stand up for what is right and just. Her lifelong commitment to helping others, despite personal hardships, serves as a powerful example of the impact one person can make on the world.

Challenges and Perseverance

Harriet Tubman's life was filled with challenges that would have deterred many people, but her perseverance and determination allowed her to rise above them all.

Enslavement

From a young age, Harriet Tubman experienced the horrors of slavery. She endured harsh treatment, witnessed the separation of families, and saw the cruelty inflicted upon her fellow enslaved people. Despite this, she never gave up hope for freedom.

Physical Injury

Harriet suffered a severe head injury as a child when a heavy metal weight struck her. This injury caused her lifelong pain, dizziness, and narcoleptic episodes. Despite these challenges, Harriet remained resilient and determined.

Constant Threat of Capture

Harriet Tubman risked her life countless times as a conductor on the Underground Railroad. Slave catchers pursued her with large bounties on her head, making each journey perilous. Despite the danger, Harriet never wavered in her mission to lead enslaved people to freedom.

Racism and Discrimination

Even after escaping slavery and settling in the North, Harriet faced racism and discrimination. She lived in a society deeply divided by prejudice, where her race made her a target for discrimination. Despite these challenges, Harriet remained steadfast in her fight for equality.

Financial Hardship

After the Civil War, Harriet struggled financially. She received only a small pension for her service, which was not enough to support herself and her family comfortably. Despite these financial hardships, Harriet continued to advocate for the rights of others.

Throughout her life, Harriet Tubman faced immense obstacles, but her determination and bravery allowed her to overcome them. She became a symbol of hope and resilience for enslaved people and all those fighting for justice and equality. Harriet Tubman's legacy teaches us the importance of perseverance in the face of adversity and the power of courage and determination to create lasting change.

The Greatest Challenge

In Harriet Tubman's courageous quest for freedom, one of the greatest challenges she faced was the Fugitive Slave Act. This law, passed in 1850, posed serious threats to enslaved people seeking freedom and made Harriet's work on the Underground Railroad even more difficult.

The Fugitive Slave Act was part of a compromise between Northern and Southern states to address the issue of slavery. This law required all citizens to assist in the capture and return of escaped enslaved individuals to their enslavers, regardless of where they were found in the

United States. It meant that even if enslaved people made it to free states like Pennsylvania or New York, they were still at risk of being captured and sent back into bondage.

For Harriet Tubman, this law intensified the danger she faced as a conductor on the Underground Railroad. The routes she traveled and the safe houses she used to shelter enslaved people were now under increased scrutiny. Slave catchers actively searched for escapees, offering rewards for their capture. Harriet knew that every journey she undertook to lead enslaved people to freedom was fraught with risk, not only for herself but for those she sought to liberate.

The impact of the Fugitive Slave Act was deeply felt by enslaved people across the country. Families who had hoped to find freedom in Northern states suddenly faced the threat of capture and forced return to slavery. The fear of betrayal by neighbors or strangers loomed large. Many enslaved individuals became more cautious, making it harder for conductors like Harriet Tubman to convince them to take the dangerous journey to freedom.

Despite these challenges, Harriet Tubman remained undeterred. She adapted her methods, becoming even more secretive and resourceful to evade capture. Harriet relied on her keen instincts and the assistance of dedicated abolitionists and sympathizers to outsmart slave catchers and ensure the safety of those she guided to freedom.

The Fugitive Slave Act highlighted the injustices of the system of slavery and spurred more people to join the abolitionist cause. It strengthened Harriet Tubman's resolve to fight for freedom and fueled her determination to challenge the oppressive laws that denied basic human rights.

Ultimately, the Fugitive Slave Act underscored the urgency of the struggle for emancipation and equality. It revealed the lengths to which those in power would go to maintain the institution of slavery. It galvanized Harriet Tubman and others to continue their courageous efforts until all enslaved people were finally liberated.

Through perseverance and bravery, Harriet Tubman defied the oppressive laws of her time and left an enduring legacy of courage and resilience. Her unwavering commitment to freedom continues to inspire people today, reminding us of the importance of standing up against injustice and fighting for the rights and dignity of all individuals.

Lessons from Harriet Tubman

Harriet Tubman's remarkable life teaches us important lessons about bravery, compassion, and determination. Let's explore seven valuable lessons inspired by the life of this extraordinary woman.

Lesson 1: Stand Up for What's Right

Harriet Tubman never backed down in the face of injustice. She stood up for her beliefs and fought tirelessly against slavery, risking her life to help others find freedom. Remember, it's important to stand up for what's right, even when it's difficult.

Lesson 2: Have Courage in Adversity

Despite facing countless challenges and dangers, Harriet Tubman never lost courage. She ventured into dangerous territories, guided others to freedom, and fearlessly fought for equality. When facing tough times, remember to summon your inner courage and persevere.

Lesson 3: Believe in Yourself

Harriet Tubman believed in herself and her abilities, even when others doubted her. She trusted her instincts and followed her convictions, achieving incredible feats. Always believe in yourself and your potential to make a positive impact on the world.

Lesson 4: Help Those in Need

One of Harriet Tubman's greatest traits was her compassion. She risked her life to help enslaved individuals escape to freedom and cared for those in need throughout her life. Learn from her example by showing kindness and helping others whenever you can.

Lesson 5: Never Give Up

Harriet Tubman faced numerous setbacks and obstacles, but she never gave up on her mission. Despite challenges, she kept moving forward with determination and resilience. Remember, persistence is key to achieving your goals.

Lesson 6: Use Your Voice for Good

Harriet Tubman used her voice to speak out against slavery and advocate for equality. You, too, can use your voice to stand up for important causes and make a difference in your community. Speak up for justice, kindness, and equality.

Lesson 7: Embrace Education and Knowledge

Harriet Tubman understood the power of knowledge. Despite being illiterate, she used her intelligence and resourcefulness to navigate perilous situations and help others. Embrace education, keep learning, and use knowledge to empower yourself and those around you.

Harriet Tubman's life is a testament to the impact one person can have on the world. By embracing these valuable lessons from her life—standing up for what's right, having courage, believing in yourself, helping others, never giving up, using your voice for good, and embracing education, you can inspire positive change and make a difference in your own unique way.

CONCLUSION

As we come to the end of this journey through the life of Harriet Tubman, we reflect on the remarkable legacy she left behind—a legacy of courage, compassion, and unyielding determination.

Harriet Tubman's story teaches us invaluable lessons about resilience and the unwavering pursuit of justice. From her early years as an enslaved child to her daring exploits on the Underground Railroad, Harriet's life exemplifies the power of individual agency in the face of adversity.

Throughout this book, we've witnessed Harriet's unwavering commitment to freedom and equality. She faced immense challenges, from the cruelty of slavery to the constant threat of capture, yet she never wavered in her resolve to fight for what was right.

Harriet's story is not just a chapter in history—it's a beacon of hope for all those who strive for a better world. Her courage inspired countless others to join the fight against injustice, and her legacy continues to inspire generations.

As we conclude this journey, let us carry forward the lessons of Harriet Tubman's life. Let us embrace the spirit of resilience, compassion, and determination that defined her character. Let us stand up against oppression and injustice, just as Harriet did, and work towards a future where all individuals are treated with dignity and respect.

May Harriet Tubman's legacy serve as a guiding light in our own quests for justice and equality. Let us honor her memory by embodying the values she held dear—values of courage, perseverance, and unwavering commitment to freedom.

Thank you for joining us on this extraordinary adventure through history. May Harriet Tubman's story continue to inspire and empower us all as we strive to create a world where everyone can live free.

Made in the USA
Middletown, DE
01 December 2024

65848784R00057